D1536214

# WHAT DO YOU SEE WHEN YOU SEE ME?

written by
JEANNIE ST. JOHN TAYLOR

illustrated by
KATHLEEN HADAM KEMLY

Equipping Kids for Life!
faithkids.com

A Faith Parenting Guide can be found on page 31.

Faith Kids® is an imprint of
Cook Communications Ministries, Colorado Springs, Colorado 80918
Cook Communications, Paris, Ontario
Kingsway Communications, Eastbourne, England

WHAT DO YOU SEE WHEN YOU SEE ME?

First printing, 2002
Printed in Singapore
1 2 3 4 5 6 7 8 9 10 Printing/Year 06 05 04 03 02

Editor: Heather Gemmen
Designer: Dana Sherrer, iDesignEtc.

Library of Congress Cataloging-in-Publication Data:

Taylor, Jeannie, 1945-
        What do you see when you see me? / written by Jeannie St. John Taylor.
            p. cm.
    Summary: On a visit to her grandmother in a nursing home, Katrina is confronted by scary old Agnes and learns that things--and people--are not always what they appear to be.
        ISBN 0-7814-3733-4
        [1. Old age--Fiction. 2. Nursing homes--Fiction. 3. Interpersonal relations--Fiction.] I. Title.

Pz7.J2146 Wh 2002
[Fic]—dc21
2001023944

To my husband, Ray, who lovingly cared for his aging parents. JSJT

For Mie Mie with love, KRK

**K**atrina peered down the hallway of the nursing home. "Please don't let mean old Agnes be awake today," she prayed.

Keeping close to the wall she took three more steps, then craned her neck to look down the hall. A wrinkled old woman with tufts of gray hair sticking out in every direction slumped in a chair near the room of Katrina's grandmother. A cane lay across the old woman's lap.

6

"Oh, no!" gasped Katrina. "She's there."

She pressed back against the wall. Her heart thumped. Her hands felt damp. "Please let her be asleep." Slowly she leaned forward and peeked around the corner. A snore as loud as a chain saw greeted her. Katrina sighed with relief.

Clutching the plate of cookies she had brought and looking straight ahead, Katrina tiptoed past old Agnes. The elderly woman gave a loud snort. Katrina froze. Without breathing, she turned her head to look at the old woman. Old Agnes' eyes were still closed. "Whew! Close call." Katrina let out her breath quietly.

She reached over and opened her grandmother's door a crack. Inside the room, she could see her grandmother napping in bed. Katrina hesitated outside the door.

9

$\mathcal{S}$uddenly, from the hallway behind her, a rasping voice asked, "What do you see when you see me?"

Katrina jumped and whirled around, nearly dropping the cookies. Old Agnes' blue eyes bore into her.

Katrina's hand slipped from the door handle. She heard her own heart hammering in her ears. Old Agnes continued to stare. The door to Grandmother's room silently swung shut.

Icy fear quivered down Katrina's spine. "Wh - what?" mumbled Katrina.

11

"What do you see when you see me?" Agnes repeated. Her shriveled mouth bunched forward. She jabbed her cane in Katrina's direction.

"I - uh…" Katrina was too scared to move away. Her feet felt glued to the floor.

"Do you see a cranky old woman with a wrinkled face?" Agnes leaned forward and thumped the tip of her cane on the tile

floor. Her eyes held onto Katrina. "Do you see twisted hands and skinny, useless legs?"

Agnes leaned even closer and her quavery voice asked again, "What do you see when you see me?"

Katrina struggled to sort out her thoughts. *I do see a cranky old woman with wrinkles,* she thought. *But it would be mean to say so.*

I didn't always look like this." Agnes adjusted herself in her chair and rested one hand on the top of her cane. "When I was your age, my cheeks glowed rosy in the summer sun. I ran through the grass barefooted. Dark curls bounced around my face."

Agnes' eyes softened. "I had a daddy, you know. At bedtime, I sat on his lap while he told me stories.

Then he tucked me in bed and tickled me before he kissed me goodnight."

Her eyes darted back to Katrina. "Is that what you see when you look at me? A little girl with a mommy and daddy who loved her?"

"Uh…" Katrina's voice stuck in her throat. She couldn't picture Agnes as a young girl with parents who loved her. She couldn't imagine anyone loving her.

I swam in the Olympics." Agnes tipped up her chin. "I didn't win, but when I arrived home, thousands of people were waiting at the docks to welcome me. They cheered and waved. A famous actor sent me flowers every day for a week—until I told him I was already in love with Harold."

Agnes no longer looked at Katrina. It was now Katrina who stared at Agnes with new eyes.

16

I married Harold two years later. In the spring. My sisters decorated the church with lilac and white lillies. Mother made my gown from satin and handmade lace and let me borrow her pearls." The old woman spoke quietly.

"Harold said my skin was softer than rose petals." Agnes' twisted fingers fluttered up to touch her withered cheek.

"We were so happy. I thought it would never end."

19

After a long silence, Agnes wiped a tear.

Katrina thought she should say something, but instead she just sat there. Waiting.

When Agnes finally spoke again, sobs choked her voice. "But the war came." Agnes dropped her head. "Harold said it was his duty to fight. He looked so handsome in his uniform. We waved good-bye."

20

The hand in Agnes' lap twitched. "I stood on the platform until his train disappeared from view. He died in the first battle of the war—saving the lives of nine of his men." The old woman gave a little shudder.

"I never remarried. I never wanted any man but Harold."

"I'm sorry," Katrina whispered.

21

That was a long time ago." Agnes sat up straighter. She dabbed at her eyes with a tissue. "Harold was a Christian man. When he and I accepted Jesus, he gave me this lovely necklace."

"I know I'll see him again in heaven. That's a great comfort to me."

*Old Agnes knows Jesus?* The thought stunned Katrina. *Wasn't she always trying to poke people with her cane? She couldn't be a Christian—could she?*

23

Agnes' voice pulled Katrina's thoughts back to the present. "My youngest son is a doctor," she said.

"He is?" Katrina's thoughts shifted, following old Agnes as she abruptly changed subjects.

"Oh yes. I'm proud of him—of both my children," Agnes said. "I taught school to support them while they were growing up. I loved my students. But my own children—why, they are more precious to me than life."

25

$D$o they visit you
a lot?" asked Katrina.

"The closest one lives
two hours away,"
Agnes said. "It's hard
for them to come to
see me because
they're so busy with
their own lives."

Agnes' blue eyes
fastened on Katrina
again. "That's why I
always wave my cane
and call out to you.
I keep hoping you'll
talk to me. You've got
the same spunk my
daughter had at
your age."

Katrina's throat tightened. She blinked back tears. "You were trying to get my attention?"

"Yes," Agnes said, "but I'm invisible to you. Just a useless old woman in a nursing home." Agnes' eyes pled with Katrina. "Is that what you see when you see me— a worthless old woman?"

27

Katrina knelt in front of Agnes. She reached for the old woman's gnarled hand and stroked it without speaking. It felt softer than rose petals.

Lifting her eyes, she gazed into Agnes' face. She looked past the wrinkles, past the brown age spots, past the sagging skin. She looked deep into the blue of the old woman's eyes. "When I look at you," Katrina said, "I see a new friend. And she's beautiful to me."

29

What Do You See When You See Me?
written by Jeannie St. John Taylor
illustrated by Kathleen Hadam Kemly
©2002 by Jeannie St. John Taylor

Equipping Kids for Life!
faithkids.com

Dear _____ ,

This is what I see when I see you:

_____

_____

_____

_____

_____

_____

_____

_____

_____

_____

Love, _____